Evangelical Methodist Church

EVANGELICAL METHODIST CHURCH
Celebrating 75 Years of Ministry

By: Dr. Jack Wease and Dr. Edward Williamson

XULON PRESS

Xulon Press
2301 Lucien Way #415
Maitland, FL 32751
407.339.4217
www.xulonpress.com

© 2021 by Dr. Jack Wease and Dr. Edward Williamson

All rights reserved solely by the author. The author guarantees all contents are original and do not infringe upon the legal rights of any other person or work. No part of this book may be reproduced in any form without the permission of the author. The views expressed in this book are not necessarily those of the publisher.

Due to the changing nature of the Internet, if there are any web addresses, links, or URLs included in this manuscript, these may have been altered and may no longer be accessible. The views and opinions shared in this book belong solely to the author and do not necessarily reflect those of the publisher. The publisher therefore disclaims responsibility for the views or opinions expressed within the work.

Unless otherwise indicated, Scripture quotations taken from the Holy Bible, New International Version (NIV). Copyright © 1973, 1978, 1984, 2011 by Biblica, Inc.™. Used by permission. All rights reserved.

Paperback ISBN-13: 978-1-6628-2503-3
Ebook ISBN-13: 978-1-6628-2504-0

Dedication

We dedicate this book to the women and men of our local churches. The founder, Dr. J. H. Hamblin, called this "a layman's denomination." The unnamed layperson ministering for decades in their local church is the champion for Christ and the heart of the Evangelical Methodist Church.

Acknowledgments

The following people contributed their time and thoughts for the printing of this book. Mrs. Teresa Grove, our secretary, typed the drafts of the early history of the book, with her eye for corrections. Several pastors and laypeople encouraged the completion of the history, along with my wife, Gilda. I give thanks to pastors and laity who offered their insights.

The cover's graphic design and website were created by Shannon Day. pumpkinpressphotography@yahoo.com

Book Orders Website
http://ed-williamson.com (book orders)

This is the authorized edition.

Foreword

In 1946, Dr. Hamblen made a statement preserved in the Historical Section of the *Discipline of the Evangelical Methodist Church,* which included the following. "The Evangelical Methodist Church came into being to preserve the distinctive doctrines of primitive Methodism...." Dr. Wease and Dr. Williamson captured the essence of this statement in their history of the EMC. Despite our ups and downs, despite our warts and faults, this purpose has remained unchanged. With its stance on Biblical holiness, the Evangelical Methodist Church remains a challenge to the world and the modern church. Our heart beats to the words of John Wesley, "The world is our parish". Whatever the future may hold, we still maintain this doctrine of Biblical holiness. The book is prophetic, accurate, verified and superbly written, and I am honored to make a statement for the book.

The final paragraphs express my thoughts with the authors.

"...The experience, understanding, and practice of scriptural holiness, which is the doctrine of entire sanctification/ baptism of the Spirit, is the Methodist Church's power. Any form of Methodism without clarity on entire sanctification has an uncertain future...."

Dr. Harold K. Thompson, Conference Superintendent, Emeritus

Preface

This written history of the Evangelical Methodist Church (EMC) focuses on the General Conference level of the denomination. In our past, we had Districts and Annual Conferences where more localized history is available.

There are heights and depths on record that provided the data and eyewitness experiences for the book's material in our seventy-five years of existence. The short history is optimistic, honest and suggests a positive hope for future ministry. The prophetic call for repentance and spiritual renewal resounds from our Methodist heritage of holiness and revival. A Third Great Awakening will be global before the Lord returns to bring in a final harvest. Fervent prayer in local churches and corporate seasons of prayer and repentance are the bedrock for the revival in the EMC.

Dr. Hamblen and the early founders loved the Methodist Church, now the United Methodist Church (UMC). Their conviction focused on people who believed in the authority of Scripture who would eventually exit the UMC. The EMC would be in position to benefit from the departure and provide a home for those wanting holiness and original Methodist doctrine and polity. Our founders did not experience the great exodus. Today we are witnessing the evangelical conservatives forming the Global Methodist Church (GMC) through the midwife of the Wesleyan Covenant Association (WCA). This exodus is a fulfillment of the vision of Dr. Hamblen and our original leaders of the EMC.

This history contains details of Covenant Church's impact upon the denomination and their spiritual journey experienced in the EMC. We acknowledge, fundamental to our movement, several churches and pastors who positively influenced the EMC, but the list is not exhaustive. The focus here is not the districts where many churches would find mention. Our focus is the *General Church*.

The question is, can we be a genuine global denomination in a worldwide digital world at this critical juncture of our history? The path for using the description *Global* requires equal representation of delegates, financial support to include international representatives, and the genuine possibility of an international person elected to the office of the general superintendent in a joint general conference for the USA and International Conferences. The EMC is not there yet, but it is the goal to become a Global Church.

Dr. Jack Wease, General Superintendent, was orally commissioned by the General Council to begin writing this historical record. After a review with Dr. Edward Williamson, he asked Dr. Williamson to finish it. The inclusion of oral tradition in conversations, and the convictions held by Dr. Hamblen and other founders, are in the flow of events. Some eyewitnesses have more information, and there will be others with their personal views of the historical events. The districts have about 35 years of historical records in their minutes.

We wanted to have unbiased historical facts with commentary on the situations and challenges faced by the Evangelical Methodist Church. The continuing greatest challenge is protecting the 'voice' and 'authority of the local church from the General Church's policies and revisions. To meet this challenge requires equal representation on the membership of the General Council and delegates to the General Conferences to protect the voice of the people. Guarding the local church's authority avoids the slippery slope into becoming a hierarchical organizational authority that replaces the integrity of the local church with episcopal domination. The goal is a transparent understanding of our past with a prophetic focus for the journey into this century.

The Early Years

The Methodist Church, during the decade of the 1940's, became further entrenched in historical criticism and liberal theology. Liberal theology and practice infiltrated the general church episcopacy, departments, Sunday school materials, and Methodist academic institutions. Dr. Hamblen experienced this drift, and resigned from the Methodist Church to pastor an independent church in Abilene, Texas.

The vision of an Evangelical Methodist Church (EMC) occurred May 9, 1946, resulting from a prayer meeting when Methodist clergy and laity gathered in Memphis, Tennessee. Dr. J. H. Hamblen was elected chairman of the forum, and became the first general superintendent of the new denomination at the first general conference later that year. The leaders shared a firm conviction that a chasm which could not be bridged existed in the Methodist Church between liberal theology and the evangelical biblical view of original Methodism. The EMC was considered a denomination for conservative Methodists to join once the definite division occurred.

At the first EMC conference in 1948, delegates wholeheartedly approved a plan presented by circuit-riding preacher Dr. Ezequiel B. Vargas, Superintendent of the Mexican Evangelistic Mission (MEM), that his conference join the Evangelical Methodist Church. Dr. Vargas and Dr. Hamblen maintained a strong friendship and working relationship. A Bible institute in Torreón, México, Instituto Bíblico Vida y Verdad, is the result of this work. Rev. Vernon and Ruth Perkins, Dr. Leroy and Kay Lindsey, Rev. Meda Jane Leach, Rev. Jack, and Sandra

Conner, Rev. Alec and Mae Hoover, Miss Ida Dixon, Rev. John, and Rev. Paula Gentry, Rev. Bill and Rev. Lisa Walker, and others served in the Mexico field. A separate history should be written for the MEM by the pastors and missionaries who have served in Mexico.

The EMC Conference adopted *The Discipline of the Methodist Episcopal Church*. The cardinal issue was the elimination of the annual conference owning and retaining the property assets of the local church and removing the practice of closing a church using the proceeds for general conference budgets. The historic mercenary confiscation of church property by the denominational hierarchy to prop up failing budgets and salaries was rejected with district by-laws by giving the proceeds from the sale of church/congregation assets to local churches' evangelism outreach, missions, and district children and youth camp ministries.

The removal of the clergy appointment system was replaced with the congregation electing the pastor of their choice. The conference coined the term congregational-connectional.

The focused on the congregational aspect secured the people's Voice and Authority for the local church in the denomination. The Methodist connectional relationship protected the voice of the local church in the general church. The authority had to rest with the local church, which would speak through the General Conference legislation. The *Discipline* revisions began in the local churches' annual church conferences. They were received directly by the General Board of Discipline Revisions (GBDR) bypassing the general council. The reason for the direct link to the GBDR and the general conference delegates was a fear of a denominational hierarchy that would seize control of local churches' proposed revisions. The local church's voice through the GBDR report would be edited or rejected before reaching the general conference floor. The general council's voice would replace the voice of the local church people and function as an hierarchical episcopal denomination.

The authority had to rest with the local church, which would speak through the general conference legislation and set the ministry priories every four years. The structure that included the judicial council that emerged in the UMC is excluded in the EMC. A judicial council functions like a US Supreme Court interpreting the US Constitution.

The general superintendent, district/conference superintendents, and councils do not have the authority to change the meaning, historical practice, and understanding of the EMC *Discipline*. The local church, through the general conference alone, has that authority.

The fear that was an elected superintendent(s) would someday try to control the general conference, pastors, and local churches through the general council and elected officials, returning to an autocratic mercenary Methodist system. The structure of the local church is not the structure of the general church, where the general superintendent is ex officio without a vote on the general boards, and the conference superintendents are not members of the boards. The goal was to protect the local churches' voice in the legislative process.

The book, *Look into Life*, by Dr. Hamblen provides the history of the denomination's origins and his autobiography. This limited historical account follows the denomination's journey by highlighting growth and governance development strategies in the structure and vision. There was a significant split between the founders over structure discussions and Wesleyan theology. Dr. W.W Breckbill and pastors walked out of the 1952 General Conference, starting another Evangelical Methodist Church. This group desired a Reformed theological interpretation of Methodism with a narrow Fundamentalist application. A court action denied the new group from using the name Evangelical Methodist Church in California. The court allowed the title EMC to be used in the other states by this group.

The EMC merged with two smaller denominations that shared its views on sanctification, grace and evangelism in its second decade. On June 4, 1960, the Evangel Church, Inc., in session at its Annual Conference, voted to unite with the Evangelical Methodist Church and become a part of the California District. Formerly known as the Evangelistic Tabernacle, and founded by Azusa Pacific College figureheads Dr. William Kirby and Dr. Cornelius P. Haggard, the denomination dates to March 27, 1933. At the time of the merger, there were eight churches; about 675 were enrolled in Sunday school, with Rev. R. Lloyd Wilson serving as president of the organization. Adopted by the Western Annual Conference of the Evangelical Methodist Church on June 22, 1960, it completed the merger.

On July 3, 1962, the General Conference of the Evangelical Methodist Church voted to merge with the People's Methodist Church, formerly known as the People's Christian Movement (PCM). The PCM came into being on January 1, 1938, with Rev. Jim H. Green of John Wesley College as the first general superintendent. The People's Methodist Church's merger finalized at a subsequent conference in the summer of 1962, approved the first step for the union. Rev. J. Neal Anderson, General Superintendent at the time of the merger, was elected Superintendent of the Virginia-North Carolina District.

On October 5, 1950, in Shelbyville, Indiana, the Evangelical Zion Methodist Church, founded by Rev. M. D. Opara of Nigeria, was received into the General Conference a membership of 10,000. This body later aligned with W.W. Breckbill's Evangelical (Independent) Methodist Conference, establishing its own organizational identity after 1952. Another Nigerian body, the Bible Methodist Church in Nigeria, consisting of around 20 congregations and a school, joined the EMC in 1974 as the Nigerian Annual Conference. This brief relationship was terminated in 1976 when missionaries determined the group had support from many denominations and groups offering financial assistance.

The denomination had seven to nine local churches surrounding the suburbs of Los Angles. Rev. Gordon Johnston pastored the church in Hollywood, where Lettie Cowan, one of the founders of One Mission Society (OMS), joined the EMC. Their stated expectation was for the Hollywood church to become a home base OMS church. In the preliminary plans, a headquarters for the mission organization would emerge. In the decades that followed, white flight from the suburbs caused many churches to relocate, merge, or close. The headquarters for OMS moved to Greenwood, IN. The 1952 General Conference approved two mission organizations to work through, World Gospel Mission and the Oriental Mission Society, now One Mission Society.

The EMC included many godly men and women who wanted to promote biblical holiness in our Wesleyan tradition in this new denomination. Our second General Superintendent, Dr. Lucian Smith, brought a passion for evangelism and fueled this DNA to reach the lost with training for the pastors. Dr. Smith wrote a paper on the episcopacy and stated the titles *Bishop* and *General Superintendent* were synonymous. Dr. Smith strategically included the structural role of the connectional within the congregational in his writings. These were useful for the church. The archives have papers written by scholars like Dr. Arthur Brestel and Dr. Fred Layman. Many others wrote reports on governance, holiness, and evangelism which are archived.

The Lord raised leaders from the EMC such as Dr. Ed Robb. Dr. Robb, mentored by Dr. Hamblen, transferred to the Methodist Church as an evangelist and impacted the UMC's renewal movement.

Dr. Cornelius Haggard joined the EMC in a merger of a small holiness group in California. In the videos of *This is the EMC*, Dr. Haggard states he believed the EMC was the *Ebenezer* (stone of help) for the EMC, saying, "Thus far has the Lord helped us." Dr. Hamblen wanted Dr. Haggard to be the next General Superintendent. The Lord directed Dr. Haggard to the Free Methodist Church where he became the President of Azua Pacific College, now a University.

The Lord raised strong leaders in the laity across the church. The laypeople became a backbone of stability for local churches. One example is Mrs. Jeanette Morris, of Sweetwater, Texas, who founded and was instrumental in the Evangelical Methodist Women's denominational ministry. Earline McDaniels in the Southern District, Mrs. Jean Thompson in the Atlantic District and Deaconess Peggy Trim, who served in many capacities in the Northwest District. Mr. Tom Wilcox of Faith Country Chapel and Mr. Kenneth and Sonya Penny of Duncanville, Texas provided strong lay leadership.

> *The Lord raised strong leaders in the laity across the church. The laypeople became a backbone of stability for the local churches.*

The most potent expression of hope from our founder's conviction was that EMC be a refuge denomination for churches and pastors from the UMC. At every General Conference of the Methodist Church (UMC) the EMC leaders anticipated an exodus. There were renewal efforts within the UMC such as the Good News Movement and others to renew and correct the drift from original Methodism in the UMC. The Evangelical United

Brethren (EUB) merger with the Methodist Church to form the United Methodist in 1968 secured all church properties owned by the Annual Conferences. The merger was opposed by many EUB pastors and congregations. The conservatives in the Northwest Conference of The Evangelical United Brethren formed their separate denomination, presently called the Evangelical Church. The EMC did not have any significant statistical growth of churches and pastors joining the denomination from the EUB. The opportunity for new churches from the UMC coming in the future was the conviction of the EMC leadership. Such a historical exodus has become a reality in 2022.

The Global Methodist (GMC) launch was May 1, 2022. Local churches, clergy, and the annual conferences can transfer and join (www.globalmethoidst.org).. The Wesleyan Covenant Association (WCA) is preparing the path for the new Methodist denomination's birth. Dr. Hamblen was 70 years early with his prophetic vision. This new movement retains original Methodist doctrine and endorses the cardinal positions of the EMC for local church ownership of property and assets and the congregation's voice in pastoral selections.

The EMC had the opportunity for inclusion in 2018 of several UMC pastors and churches waiting on our doorstep. These new churches would double the size of the EMC, fulfilling Dr. Hamblen's vision. WCA considered joining the EMC, which became an impossibility with the WCA growing into the millions of members and hundreds of churches for the new denomination for 2022. The founders' vision of the EMC as the refuge for churches leaving the UMC is obsolete with the formation of the Global Methodist Church. We explore the unfulfilled dream and affirm securing a future for the EMC.

> *The founders' vision of the EMC as the refuge for churches leaving the UMC is obsolete with the formation of the Global Methodist Church.*

The Seventies

The decade of the 1970s produced three main themes: evaluation, evangelism and expansion. Dr. Hamblen had envisioned and promoted a global vision for the denomination. There was no influx of pastors and churches from the United Methodist Church to increase our numbers. The denomination utilized the church growth movement from the seventies into the eighties to grow the local church.

As the Evangelical Methodist Church neared its 25th anniversary, there was concern over the denomination's growth or lack thereof. The EMC illustrated that concern with the proposals at the 1970 General Conference held in St. Louis.

One proposal would streamline the EMC leadership positions into two annual conferences and the nine district conferences into four annual conferences. A full-time annual conference superintendent presides for the individual conferences. The annual conference superintendent position would make unnecessary the positions of assistant general superintendents and the nine district superintendents. Another proposal concerned dropping the Methodism tradition of deacons' orders and retaining the elders' orders. The General Conference passed both proposals. A special, called general conference was slated for the following year to consider boundary proposals of the four new annual conferences. However, two-thirds of the local churches failed to approve the conference restructuring plan. There was agreement on the elimination of the clergy Deacons' Orders. Even though the restructuring plan failed adoption, evaluation of the EMC's structure continued.

In 1973, the Eastern Annual Conference merged five districts into three by joining the East Central and Great Lake Districts and the Mid-south and Southeast Districts. These two new districts joined the Atlantic District, and all three were to have full-time district superintendents. At this Conference and the Western Annual Conference, the districts met for business at the annual conference site for the first time. These changes using the term Annual Conference aligned with the traditional Methodism structure and secured the denomination's connectional aspect. The new system was attractive to the conservative United Methodists who eventually exited from the liberal wing of their denomination.

The EMC hired Christian Service Fellowship (CSF) to evaluate the denomination and provide suggestions to continue the efforts for reorganization. The following are quotes and summaries of the report:

'The world has changed, is changing, and will change. Its solidarity and effectiveness are a matter of concern. Proper structure and updating are necessary and must not be an 'unspiritual exercise.' The study offered the following alternatives:

1. Do nothing. Remain the status quo, live in the mediocrity.
2. Dissolve. Let each congregation go its way to whatever fellowship it may.
3. Re-group. Keep the church essentially the way it is except to redraw geographical and authority lines so that there is a higher and more efficient degree of compatibility among the various groupings/participants.
4. Restructure. More than re-groupings, the General Conference calls for a re-definition of roles and structural relationships. Include the reasons why the EMC believes Methodist connectionism and congregationalism are compatible in the organizational structure.
5. Merge. Answer the questions: With Whom? On what terms? At what speed? With what ultimate date? *Does merge mean, be swallowed up or create a different third group from two or more existing groups?*

Viewed idealistically, CSF suggests an alternative (4) as a test to the EMC regarding whether the denomination has deeply rooted relationships among and between the congregations, the ministers and lay leaders; relationships that can endure proper restructuring which produces growth spiritually, numerically at home and abroad.

The gravest issue of the report is the congregational-connectional hybrid of being a congregational independent based denomination or a connectional episcopal denomination. The present model's structure is a seedbed for endless controversy over which structure dominates the other. The option to 'dissolve' (2) the denomination and allow churches to join other groups or associations of churches has been chosen by local EMC congregations over the decades.

The founders copied the Methodist Episcopal Church's Discipline for the EMC *Discipline,* minus ownership of local church property by the Annual Conference and *Bishop* clergy appointments of pastors to the local churches. Although the EMC is on paper 95% connectional, the 5% of congregationalism dominated the denomination. The EMC is congregational only in owning their property and selecting their pastor. The governance is connectional in the Methodist tradition. The reality was that (5) merger might be the most promising option.

The CSF report also recommended a Planning Commission with two task forces: a Task Force on Re-structure and a Task Force on Merger. The delegates implemented the report at the 19th session of the General Conference held at the Southern-Peabody Hotel in Memphis, Tennessee, in June of 1974.

The pitfalls examined in the CSF report proved accurate in the coming decades. There was an independent spirit and disconnect among the local churches, pastors, and the general church. The lack of connection fostered ambitious aspirations for positions and control in the districts and general church. The was an influx of pastors, with no historical allegiance and understanding of the EMC or Methodism, who were allowed into pulpits with minimal theological education and no introduction to the EMC.

The EMC historian, Dr. William Dean, professor at Olivet Nazarene University, observed, the EMC adopted the Methodist Episcopal Discipline with the educational requirements, but then adopted the Methodist Church South emphasis on 'being called' as the only requirement for pastoral ministry. Theological education without the Spirit's anointing fails the church. A person called of God and full of the Holy Spirit will produce converts and church growth, which may be a mile wide and an inch deep. The creation of the Haggard School of Ministry in the EMC provides theological training for our bi-vocational clergy, thus addressing this concern for pastoral preparation and training.

The fever of congregationalism dominated the landscape. Local churches and district conferences engaged in undermining pastors' and leaders' character and ministry, then recruiting people to vote for change. Local churches and pastors experienced this predicted pitfall (CSF Report). At times whole conferences experienced a busload of recruited delegates to vote in a block on issues and superintendents. Examples are the 1986 Mid-Sates District Conference; 2010 Atlantic District Conference; 1962, 1976, 2010, and 2018 General Conferences.

The congregational-connectional system fostered divisions. The *Methodist Episcopal Book of Discipline* was the *EMC Discipline*. Despite the congregational aspects of property and calling of the pastor being inserted, the denomination operated as an congregational association of independent churches.

The levels of organization are the local church, the annual/district conferences and at the top, is the general conference. The general conference continued during these years to refine the congregational/connectional structure. These godly leaders desired to see effective local church ministry affirming the local church as the foundation of the denomination. After serving as General Superintendent for twelve years, Dr. Ralph Vanderwood resigned from the position.

> *These godly leaders desired to see effective local church ministry affirming the local church as the foundation of the denomination.*

The newly elected General Superintendent Lloyd Garrett was also quite interested in evaluation and restructuring. After extensive study of the denomination, General Superintendent Garrett announced a special called General Conference in 1976 to consider several essential items concerning restructuring. His first proposal was to combine the district and annual conferences, making each district conference a district annual conference. The plan passed. Dr. Garrett was committed to the ministry of the local church as the foundation of the EMC. This approved plan deposited the decision making assembly closer to the local church, not in the general church elected officers.

The second item proposed passed: General Conference will meet every two years instead of every four years. But the most radical proposal was eliminating the office of general superintendent and forming a board of superintendents, which would be composed of the district-annual superintendents. This would unify the denominational leadership for recommending ministry priorities for the denomination and fostering the Methodist connectional fellowship. This also protects the denomination from the hierarchical empowerment of the general church elected positions of treasurer, secretary and general council.

While this proposal was under consideration, the Task Force on Re-structure was allowed to give its report. They proposed to retain the office of general superintendent but to detail the job description of that office. So the conference was faced with the decision to maintain or discontinue the office of the general superintendent. When it came time to vote on the motion to terminate the office, 116 voted yes and 86 voted no. So the proposal received a majority vote but failed to obtain the required three-fourths majority for a constitutional revision.

Dr. Garrett's last proposal passed: "that a comprehensive review of every office and program be conducted to determine the relationship between cost and productivity, and that each office or program continue in the light of this evaluation." There is no record of a motion or vote on the Eastern and Western Annual Conferences' dissolution or creation of district-annual conferences. However, nine districts were formed and began to function based upon Dr. Garrett's proposal.

The unexpected resignation of Dr. Garrett as the General Superintendent placed the special called Conference into turmoil.

Delegates began forming voting blocks for their favorite candidate of the two nominees, Rev. John Kunkle, a missionary with WGM Bolivia who was the conference speaker, and Dr. Neil Anderson, pastor of Parkersburg, WV, President emeritus of John Wesley College and former General Superintendent of the People's Methodist Church. In a narrow vote, the Conference elected Rev. John Kunkle.

Evangelism was another primary concern for the 1970s. It got off to a good start at the 1970 General Conference with the ESP's approval (Expanding Spheres Plan). ESP built on Acts 1:8, "But ye shall receive power, after that the Holy Ghost comes upon you: and ye shall be witnesses unto me both in Jerusalem, and in all Judea, and Samaria, and unto the uttermost part of the earth."

Rev. James Mumme summarized the plan. "The Expanding Spheres Plan is simply an application of the teaching of Acts 1:8. It seeks to 1) mobilize all the believers and their resources, 2) within the framework of the church, 3) to reach all the unbelievers in the area, 4) through every available means."

The first part of the plan was Operation Inner Circle. Once again, Rev. Mumme gave an overview. "Operation Inner Circle is a six-month emphasis on obtaining the extra spiritual power that is needed (Acts 1:8) to drive a saturation evangelism effort in the area surrounding each Evangelical Methodist Church in the United States."

General Superintendent Vanderwood expanded upon the first phase and outlined the entire program. "The first phase of the ESP is 'Operation Inner Circle,' dealing particularly with our hearts and churches. The stated purposes are: (1) to strengthen personal relations to Christ; (2) to strengthen relationships within the church, giving attention to those activities and attitudes which bring forth love for one another and encourage others to grow in the knowledge and grace of Jesus Christ and (3) strengthen relations with non-Christians to 'build bridges' over which we might take Christ to them."

For the year 1971, prayer, Bible study and Scripture memorization were emphasized. "The schedule for the ESP, following the completion of 'Operation Inner Circle, is as follows: 'Operation Jerusalem,' January through June 1972; 'Operation Judea,' July through December 1972; January through December 1973; 'Operation Samaria,' July through December 1973; and 'Operation Uttermost,' January through July 1974."

Another evangelism thrust originated from the Board of Home Missions and Church Extension. The March 1970, issue of the *Voice* summarized a General Council meeting. A survey of the EMC's growth was reviewed and determined that an emphasis should focus upon evangelism and church extension.

Dr. Fred Layman, the chairman of the Board of Home Missions and Church Extension, outlined the "Church Extension Plans for the 70's" in the May 1970, issue of the *Voice*. The adopted slogan was MISSION 70's: Seventy New Churches In this Decade." The financial support for this project would come from three primary sources:

1. Evangelical Methodist Builders, a new name for the old Helping Hand program. The EM Builders sought 1000 supporters who would agree to give $5 per appeal with a limit of four requests annually.
2. J.H. Hamblen Loan Fund would loan more significant amounts than the $5000 from the previous fund. Its sources of support would come from gifts, bequests, and investors. Guarantee Loan Fund—would guarantee repayment to commercial lenders if a local EMC should default.

This board also proposed creating a church extension resources file at Headquarters. It also suggested quarterly offerings for church extension, not just the traditional Thanksgiving offering. There was also an appeal for larger established EMCs to *mother* new churches, and a final appeal to bathe the whole matter in prayer. The 1970 General Conference adopted this church extension program. All denominational financial requests exclude the Easter season to avoid infringing upon local church unique offerings. The historic denomination policies and the future districts reaffirmed that all assets received from the closing of churches are restricted for evangelism and church planting. They were determining that the assets of a closed church used for planting a new church honors the dedication of the laity who invested years in their local church. The funds are never withdrawn to support a general fund or salaries of superintendents. It is a historical fact that when funds are lacking, leadership will seek to use those restricted funds. Evangelism is the point of the lifeline of ministry in the EMC, and these historical policies protect the funding for evangelism and new churches.

The Board of Church Extension proposed a Silver Anniversary Project at the special General Conference of 1971. The General Council had suggested the Church Extension Board present such a project to the General Conference. The project was to plant a new EMC in a large metropolitan area. The conference raised approximately $7500 for that project.

By early 1972, the General Council had approved a plan to plant a church in the Cincinnati area. The General Board of World Missions authorized Several survey trips. It was determined to concentrate on the growing Northwest edge of Cincinnati. For two years, the East Central District Conference voted to raise part-time pastoral support, for $200 per month. Survey teams from Asbury College, Asbury Seminary, Southland EMC in Lexington, and the EMC in Covington, Kentucky and Columbus, Indiana contacted 1500 homes in the area to determine interest. Rev. Charles Liles received the appointment to pastor the new church.

The first service convened on September 10, 1972, with sixteen present and the potential for many more. However, Rev. Liles slipped a disc in his back. That persistent pain added to his continuing education at Asbury Seminary persuaded him to resign a month later. The pastoral search and appeal to the clergy for a pastor proved fruitless. The Cincinnati church plant project closed in November of that same year. Even though this effort did not produce spectacular results, its inception illustrated the emphasis on evangelism.

The evangelism emphasis continued throughout the '70s through widely publicized and well-attended evangelism workshops. The first workshop was held in Ft. Worth, Texas, in September 1977, with Rev. John Maxwell as the chief speaker. Rev. Maxwell's church in Lancaster, Ohio, had the fastest-growing Sunday School in Ohio the previous year. Over three days, Maxwell conducted eight one-hour lectures on church growth and soul-winning strategies. The evening services left all inspired and ready to do God's business. The success of this workshop prompted the EMC's first Congress on Evangelism in September 1979. John Maxwell returned as a speaker along with "Mr. Sunday School", Dr. Elmer Towns. Once again, all the participants received not only information but the inspiration to win lost souls.

The decade of the 1970s experienced expansion with the vision for global ministry. This expansion came with missionary involvement, an extended youth ministry, a new headquarters building and the new stewardship and development service. The Hamblen/Brunner new headquarters, in Wichita, Kansas, required all elected General Conference officers to reside in Wichita.

The missions' expansion extended into new fields, with the appointment of more missionaries and an additional airplane for Bolivia's ministry.

One of the new fields was an ongoing work in Nigeria. In March of 1973, the Board of World Missions considered helping this work in Nigeria. The plan included aiding a conference of fifteen churches to train its ministers at World Gospel Mission's Kenya Highlands Bible College. Later that year, the Board of World Missions sent $1000 to Nigeria as a deposit with the Nigerian government to allow three college students to remain there for further training. At the 19th General Conference held in Memphis, Tennessee, "It was moved that we merge with the Bible Methodist Church in Nigeria (as the Nigerian Annual Conference). Seconded and carried." The August-September 1974 issue of the *Voice* gave a further description of the Nigerian work. The field consisted of twenty churches, plus a high school that planned to enroll 250 students. The campus included six completed buildings, with three unfinished buildings. There were also eight new church buildings under construction for the latest congregations.

The *Voice's* next issue carried an appeal for two of the high school buildings' finances for roofs. Included were pictures of the EMC supported students with a request to take out shares for their further education.

By the end of 1974, questions arose about the denomination's involvement with this group were. Rev. Lewis Hedges, an EMC missionary who served as a WGM missionary to Burundi, Africa, was asked to visit the site and evaluate it. News from Nigeria still appeared in the *Voice* the following year. Early in 1976, the Board of World Missions voted to terminate our affiliation with the Nigerian work. It seems that the group was receiving funds not only from the EMC but also from any group that could provide the needed finances.

The EMC mission work expanded into Bolivia. Rev. John Kunkle provided the needed push to establish this work in Bolivia. Rev. John and Mabel Kunkle served as WGM missionaries to Bolivia for many years. At the 1974 General Conference, John Kunkle became the new Director of World Missions. In the October-November 1974 issue of the *Voice,* Rev. Kunkle described his mission's philosophy in an article entitled, *Where Do We Go from Here?* In this article, Rev. Kunkle states, "In the undertaking of new missionary tasks around the world, we shall endeavor, as a general policy, not to 'build on another man's foundation.' We plan to start from the ground up, with only very rare exceptions."

By May of 1975, Rev. Kunkle announced in the *Voice,* "November 12-25 will find the members of the Explorers Club in Bolivia, where they will be checking out several possible sites for the new work."

Members of the first Operation Exploration to Bolivia included Rev. John Kunkle, Rev. Jack Wease, Carl Thompson, Larry Cullum, and Marvin Warehime. They were impressed with the gospel's need and receptivity to the gospel on some of the ranches they visited. Early in 1976, the Board of World Missions approved Bolivia as an EMC mission field and placed Ron and Mary Ann Walker under full appointment to the new field. The Walkers were laypeople from the EMC in Sullivan, Indiana. Larry and Becky Cullum, from the Memphis, Tennessee EMC were placed under appointment to Bolivia later that same year.

The second tour of Bolivia occurred on November 20- December 6, 1976. This team included John and Mabel Kunkle, Ralph Vanderwood, Larry and Becky Cullum, Ron Walker, Alex Hoover, Marvin Warehime, Tim Hicke, Arthur Brestel, Burch Surbrook. Larry Lindahl met them in Bolivia and served as translators. Arthur Brestel, who served as editor of the denominational magazine, wrote an inspirational summary of the tour in the January- February 1977 issue. He described the opportunities he witnessed on the trip: "The Siriono tribe is a persecuted, neglected, suffering, diminishing tribe, probably about a thousand in number, scattered in the jungle, very much in need of the gospel and of medical care and other necessities of life. Here is an open field, a great need that the Evangelical Methodist Church needs to consider answering. As I listened to the need and the desperate time in which the Siriono have fallen, I constantly remembered J.H. Hamblen's constant message to the EMC, 'Perhaps thou art come to the kingdom for such a time as this.' Dr. Hamblen and other founders expected the EMC to become a dominant worldwide voice of Methodism. The Board of World Missions believed the EMC 'for such a time as this' to bring salvation to the Siriono Indians. Later in the trip, the team visited the ranch country, held services, and was privileged to see a couple come to Christ."

This experience, as well as the entire trip, prompted this appeal from Rev. Brestel: "The Evangelical Methodist Church has a great field before us. Our field is an area of ranches scattered through the jungle where there is no Christian work Catholic or Protestant. We now have converts, babes in Christ already converted under our ministry- babes in Christ with no Sunday School to go to, no worship services to attend, no pastor to guide them, no mature Christian to go for counsel. How long can these babes needing the 'sincere milk of the word' survive and grow with no one to give them the milk? These souls are your responsibility and my responsibility now. God has given them to us. We as a church must act, and we must act now." These words reflected the Spirit of the EMC to get involved in Bolivia.

Ed and Joan Rodman were a welcome addition to the Bolivian work, veteran missionaries to the Bolivian highlands. They joined the First EMC in Wichita, Kansas, and applied to the Board of World Missions for placement in Bolivia. Joan was the principal of the American High School in La Paz, the Bolivian capital. They had served for several years in that area, establishing work for a sister denomination. That work had become indigenous, and the Rodmans wished to help the EMC establish a ministry in that area. The EMC claimed Boliva for Chirst with the Rodmans in the highlands and the new preaching point in the lowlands.

The May-June issue of the *Voice* in 1977 reported the progress in preparing for Bolivia with the Rodmans' appointment to Bolivia. Since Joan received pay as the American school principal, only Ed needed to raise Bolivia's necessary shares. Larry Lindahl came under preliminary appointment to the Bolivian field. Larry was quite familiar with the language and culture since his parents had been missionaries to Bolivia with WGM for many years. His training as an airplane pilot also made him a valuable candidate.

Rev. Kunkle outlined plans for Bolivia in this mission's article:

> "Preliminary contacts with the government have been made, and steps are being taken for us to be recognized in Bolivia as a legitimate evangelical body... A work tour is being planned to Bolivia in the Fall of 1977 to prepare housing for our new missionaries. Their work concentrated in the ranch country of northern Bolivia. They are living temporarily in Riberalta until a permanent site for the base of operation can be established. There is a unanimous feeling that an airplane is necessary for an effective outreach in that primitive territory. Let us pray that every need will be met!"

Ron and Mary Ann Walker's appointment to ministry in Bolivia was strategic for the mission. Ron conducted the ministry with the airplane and Mary contributed with her musical talent. These two were the gifted church planters in Bolivia.

The December 1977 issue of the Voice records Rev. Kunkle's thoughts on Operation Exploration III's results to Bolivia. He reiterated a need for the Bolivian work. "The small plane is essential to the effective reaching of the ranch and village country. We need it just about one year from now on the outside, and sooner if possible. We have talked about it, and some have given a little bit toward the project so that there is about $3000.00 or a little over in the fund. This is a start, but just barely. Now it is time to find out how much various churches and individuals will do during the next twelve months, so we can begin planning. What is your commitment to the task, either by cash or faith promise?"

It became evident that the plane was a necessity for the Bolivian ministry. A trip that would take days via the river would take only a few hours by plane. A plane would also provide a practical means of ministry by carrying passengers or cargo to isolated areas. Regular appeals occurred in the *Voice* for the airplane ministry. A list of airplane parts and their cost was listed so an individual, Sunday School class or church could work toward purchasing that particular part of the plane.

Additional exploratory trips to Bolivia were made in 1978 by Rev. John Kunkle, Dr. Jack Wease, Ed Rodman, Marvin Warehime, and Emil Caldwell. Later in that same year, the Board of World Missions sent $1500 to the Rodmans to purchase property in Bolivia on the Alto Plano for a local group to build a church.

An encouraging step the following year happened when Larry and Becky Cullum made the journey to Bolivia to start the new work. Larry, a member of the first exploration trip to Bolivia in 1975, reported God spoke to his heart about serving there. In the Fall of 1976, Larry and Becky were both members of Operation Exploration II. That trip convinced them that God was calling them to Bolivia. They returned home to Covington, Tennessee, and Larry sold his thriving plumbing business. After several months on their deputation and then language school in Costa Rica, the Cullums left for Bolivia on January 19.

In addition to the new work in Bolivia, the EMC maintained the work in the Mexican field. The January-February 1976 issue of the *Voice* reported that the Wease Memorial Church's first floor was up and roofed. The second floor was to be worked on by a crew of volunteers on an April trip to Mexico. The new church building was dedicated to the memory of Evangeline and Jacque Wease, wife and daughter of Jack Wease, who died in separate auto accidents.

Later that year, the General Board of World Missions voted to reopen the Life and Truth Bible Institute, and appointed Meda Jane Leach to the Mexican field. She was in language school by 1978. The Life and Truth Bible Institute celebrated its first graduate in 1979. Also, near the end of the decade, Jack and Sandra Conner and their family joined the Life and Truth Bible Institute staff. Dr. Leroy and Kay Lindsay served in Mexico, establishing foundational work for theological education. Their vision was to have a seminary for our pastors and expansion in the form of a ministry to the Tarahumara Indians. Rev. John Kunkle described Operation Exploration to the Tarahumara land: "When we left San Juanito, we moved into the heart of Tarahumara land, the part that is little touched by modern civilization. We received a warm welcome from nearly all these gentle, timid, quiet people. They urged us to come to help them, and one chief, in particular, said, 'It is important that you come. We need the message of God.'

We do many of the things we do because no one ever taught us differently.' The government officials were cordial and made us welcome to enter the area for missionary work. Such a wide-open door must be entered quickly. Will you do your part? We saw the desperate need, spiritual, physical, and economic. God help us to join with our Mexican brethren in meeting these needs." In 1977 Rev.Vernon Perkins reported on the second Tarahumara Trek. Rev. Alex and Mae Hoover had answered God's call to minister to the Tarahumara, but Rev. Perkins saw a more immediate need. "With the preparation of the Alex Hoover family for precisely that purpose, 'to explain more' to the Tarahumaras, we trust that the EMC family will continue to pray for these people so in need of the gospel. It'll be in the summer of 1979 before the Hoovers will be able to take up residency in the mountains. Meanwhile, what will be our part in the evangelization of the Tarahumara people? Pray that there will be someone willing to take them the gospel NOW, showing them the Lord's way in walking in holiness and power."

> *"When we left San Juanito, we moved into the heart of Tarahumara land, the part that is little touched by modern civilization."*

The EMC's expansion efforts were not limited to foreign fields. The Board of Youth Activities saw the need for a full-time director to concentrate on EMC's youth needs. Vernon Perkins, who was on furlough from his usual ministry in Mexico, was appointed Director for the 1973-74 school year. In October 1974, Rev. Jack Conner became the new Director. In the January 1978 issue of the *Voice*, the new Director spelled out the three main goals of the Evangelical Methodist Youth. The first goal was to distribute good literature.

The Board of Youth Activities evaluated an immense amount of literature. It made recommendations to the local churches' EMY best literature for youth. The second goal was to hold Leadership Training Seminars (LTS) in different areas of the country. Jack Conner describes the first Leadership Training Seminar: "The first such LTS was held in February at the Old Richmond EMC in Tobaccoville, North Carolina.

Forty five participants profited from workshops presented by Rev. Ben Church (Atlantic District Youth Director) and Mrs. Carol Friday (Pastor's wife from High Point EMC) as well as myself. Workshops were 45 minutes in length with breaks for lunch and fellowship. Many in attendance went away enthused with new possibilities for youth ministry."

The EMY's third goal was to have a Hamblen Student Center adjacent to each college. Sizable groups of EMCers attended Azusa and Vennard. The first Hamblen Student Center was located near Vennard College in University Park, Iowa. The EMY also emphasized a program that had been influential for many Years, the Youth Challenger program. A church would commit to supporting a youth worker for a summer. The church would benefit by gaining an extra worker for various ministries in the church, while the worker would benefit by gaining some real-life experience working in a local church. Unfortunately, due to a lack of finances, the full-time director position for the Board of Youth Activities had to be dropped.

The January-February 1977 issue of the *Voice* outlined the services of Mr. Ray Lyne, president of Commonwealth Foundation. "Mr. Lyne will be working directly with our church in four basic areas: (1) To help to develop a long-term program of financial security and provide for expansion in the areas of church planting, missionary ministries, and education. (2) To assist in developing a training program for our leadership in the areas of financial development. (3) To conduct seminars on estate planning and charitable giving for the membership of our local churches. (4) To assist our membership in the area of estate analysis, and recommendations for the most effective planning of charitable estates."

The Eighties and Nineties

These two decades experienced several local churches across the country, both small and large with growth and influence for the denomination and the Kingdom. This list is not exhaustive.

The Duval Church which in Washington State, multiplied under the leadership of Rev. Chester and Penny Kwait. The Macon Church in Georgia, grew with Rev. Floyd B'Hymer and Rev. Tim Long, Several pastors estasbished the Cedar Ridge Church in Duccanville, Texas, that provided effective leadership for the district, St. Charles Church in Missouri, made grew under several pastors into an effective ministry. The church plant, Crossroads, in Nampa, Idaho by the Northwest District with Rev, Jim and Rev. Dori Halbert has become a leader in the denomination for missions and misitry. The Stockton, CA, church Rev. Al Barret all had a positive influence of leadership in the California District.. The Elizabeth City church in North Carolina, with Dr. Cruse, Rev. Warren Banks, and Dr. Art Wilt, impacted the denomination in missions and evangelism. Faith Country Chapel in New Castle, PA, provided a strong lay leadership for the Conference and was planted by Dr. Lloyd Garett.

The small historic church in San Diego, CA deserves mention due to it's unique ministry, that evolved from the 1990s through today. The Lefler family were key leaders in this church and focused the church on missions, especially in Mexico. In the late 90s the ministry evolved into serving and outreach to the homeless and youth in the Bay area. The church is located on a strategic triangle in San Diego. The fellowship hall was turned into a gym with a ministry of Boxers for Christ reaching many young men from the streets of San Diego.

A greater ministry was to the homeless, in fact a person who had been homeless was converted and pastored the church becoming an Elder in the EMC. Their Sunday morning attendance with the predominately homeless people, drug addicts, etc., fluctuated from month to month. The point here is this small church in our small denomination makes an impressive ministry impact in a major USA city. The San Diego church ministry reaches some of the people Jesus misses the most. There are other small churches like Abilene, whose ministry to the mentally and physically challenged fulfills the call of the gospel. The EMC denomination is small, but we have unique ministries in local churches reaching their communities for Christ.

There has been throughout its history, the exodus of churches from the EMC. In contrast with the UMC ownership of the property are EMC local congregation could withdraw with their property at any time. When a local church's vision no longer aligned with the EMC's vision and ministry, the appropriate authority released the church with their property. At times, following disciplinary procedures or by the act of the general conference or council were released upon the request of the congregation. A partial list of exodus are Columbia, SC; Macon, GA; Ridgefield, WA and Casta Grande, AZ. There were threats from the largest district leaving the EMC to form their own associations.

The Bethel Methodist Church Association resulted from a theological disagreement in the EMC Mid-States District. Four churches left the EMC. The National Association of Wesleyan Evangelicals was formed following the consolidation of EMC districts in the 2010 General Conference. It is composed of eight former Southern District EMC churches in Tennessee, Georgia and Arkansas. The General Council disaffiliated these churches.

There were also positive attitudes toward mergers with like-minded denominations. These attitudes aligned with the recommended step for the survival of the denomination from the consultants. Avoiding mediocrity in ministry required a union with another denomination. The commissioning of the 1982 task force chaired by Rev. Warren Banks was tasked with formulating a formal merger with The Churches of Christ in Christian Union (CCCU). This is a sister denomination to the EMC and reciprocal observers are invited to each one's general conferences. This merger was 95% complete and would have given the EMC the dream of many, a Bible College in Circleville, Ohio, which today is Circleville Christian University. The General Conference was following the CSF recommendations that a merger was vital for the denomination's survival. The congregational view dominated the EMC, influencing policy and local churches. The EMC never recovered that future from the failure to merge with CCCU.

The Atlantic District extended into an international ministry. Dr. Charles Church, Superintendent of the Atlantic District, our largest with 40+ local churches, promoted church extension. Dr. Church's heart was with the Indian Cave Youth Camp in Virginia. The Superintendent, Dr. Harold Thompson, advanced and established ethnic church ministries and secured funding for the new Myanmar mission field buildings. Rev. David Hayes and his wife Cathy provided funds for two large structures at Tahan headquarters in the following years.

In 1984, Dr. Edward Williamson and his wife, Loretta, planted a new independent Covenant Church in Morgantown, WV. The unbiblical stance on human sexuality launched a church planting movement in North Central WV. Covenant chose to affiliate with the EMC during the early stages while renting the Ramada Inn for worship services in Morgantown, WV. The reasons for selecting the EMC were twofold: Dr. Hamblen's vision of eventually being the refuge for the departure from the UMC, and the biblical example set by the Atlantic District Superintendent, Dr. Charles Church.

Dr. Church's superintendent ministry was in stark contrast to that of the UMC. The latter performed their duties like a CEO in a Methodist spiritual wrapper. There was never a move of the Spirit when they preached at the local church. The experience with Dr. Church was biblical preaching, conversions at the altar, healing the sick, and building up of the church. An additional affirmation burned in our hearts upon hearing Rev. John Kunkle, General Superintendent (Bishop), preach on the atonement and the blood of Christ for the redemption of the world. Covenant was blessed to be in this relationship and consequently experienced ministry growth that has lasted to this day.

Covenant planted a Christian School and five local churches in North Central WV. The church birthed a children's camp, Spring and Fall youth retreats, for the northern regions of the Atlantic District. In 1998 their Easter Services had 758 in worship.

General Superintendent Clyde Zehr encouraged the General Board of Evangelism to hold Church Growth Seminars in the nine districts. This emphasis upon church planting and multiplication laid a foundation for the next century's expansion of the USA's denomination. Rev. Zehr and Mr. John Pedersen brought financial funding to launch the church plant in Nampa, ID. Dr. Williamson, chairing the General Board of Evangelism, provided care and preaching at the newborn church plant in the small Baptist Church, which Rev. Jim Halbert and church leadership had acquired. Dr. Williamson later cared for the pastor and staff in a devastating church split that could have destroyed this young church.

The 2000 Decades
1998-2013

Dr. Jack Wease was elected in 1994 as the General Superintendent. He completed the enormous task of moving the International Headquarters from Wichita, Kansas to Indianapolis, Indiana. Indiana was strategic in placing the general conference officers and offices central to EMC local churches' most heavily populated areas. Dr. Wease and General Secretary Vernon Perkins were responsible for moving the assets to Indianapolis. The Shelbyville EMC hosted the temporary office until the purchase of land or a building in Indianapolis.

In July 1996, the new Headquarters' dedication in Indianapolis took place during the 25th anniversary of the EMC founding. Dr. Wease and Dr. Williamson talked about the 1998 General Conference and the General Superintendent's election. They concurred that Dr. Arthur Wilt was God's choice for this office, chair of the Board of Advanced Education and Ministerial Studies. Mid-quadrennium, the circumstances were changing, and Dr. Wilt's availability was no longer certain. The discussion included the availability of Dr. Williamson in the nominations. The men prayed together.

The following is from Dr. Williamson's notes: "I prefer for Dr. Wease to continue in office if Dr. Wilt is no longer available. My brother Art Wilt would make the best General Superintendent the EMC ever had." I honor friends and pastors who shared many cautions and reasonable considerations for Loretta and me and Covenant in making this decision. Loretta and I founded Covenant (1984) and Covenant Christian School, which is most difficult to leave. There is long-term security both financially and in ministry growth in staying in the local church. The move would require a severe salary reduction to assume this office.

The church reached 750 in worship on Resurrection Sunday.

Brother pastors reminded me of the dangers of submitting my ministry and future to a general conference. Conferences are very unpredictable in the EMC, but your local church will stand with you as their founding pastor through retirement years.

Dr. Lloyd Garrett, former General Superintendent, called me on Sunday morning. I was announcing the departure from Covenant to Indianapolis. His words gave me great comfort: Ed, I observed you over the years, and I see you are not serving as the GS out of ambition, but out of obedience.' Dr. Garrett opposed having the office of a General Superintendent, so these words were gratifying to Loretta and me.

Dr. Williamson's background of being raised in the Evangelical United Brethren and the United Methodist Church, and serving in their clergy, brought understanding to governance and structure. He served on the Board of Trustees of Asbury University during the Board's governance restructure. Dr. Williamson chaired the Board of One Mission Society (OMS) in their ten-year transition into a truly global mission organization in this new day of internationalization. The District Superintendents' focus was church multiplication/discipleship and preparing the denomination to receive local churches from the UMC when the great division would occur. The conviction is the hope and dream of our founders.

Dr. Williamson emphasized adherence to the *Discipline*,. "You are the General, and you can interpret the *Discipline* and take action as you see fit" was a common phrase. The statement was rejected by Dr. Williamson, stating the general superintendent's office carries out the rules of the *Discipline* following the traditional understanding, interpretation, and practice over the years. The offices of general superintendent and the general council have limited power restricted to implementing the programs and directives of the general conference. The UMC has a Judicial Council, much like the US Supreme Court, to interpret the *Discipline* between sessions of the general conference.

The EMC has no judicial council, and must wait until the next general conference for clarifications and revisions. The following summary points describe the ministry during this period

- The ten local churches and pastors that promised the most significant potential for planting a daughter church were invited to Indianapolis in 2000 for visioning and prayer. Dr. Charles Lake of the Community Church of Greenwood hosted a luncheon, sharing the practical considerations for launching a daughter church. The EMC, over the next several years, planted several new churches.
- The Department of Multicultural Ministry was created to train local churches and pastors, with ethnic ministers among the immigrants coming to the USA worldwide.
- General boards were not functioning, with one Board not reporting or meeting for the entire four years quadrennium. The district boards had no general church uniform ministerial credenting of pastors for ordination.
- The corrections occurred in 2010 by combining district boards and functions into one general board for each area.
- The General Board of Finance purchased a machine for the General Secretary to digitize the General Conference's historical Minutes and other important documents/reports. General Board of Finance Chair Mr. Stanley Morris led the denomination with a balanced budget, securing a clean financial audit. His foresight set up the Hamblen-Brunner Endowment Fund when the EMC received one million dollars from the Brunner estates. The endowment retained 80%

The offices of General Superintendent and the general council have limited power restricted to implementing the programs and directives of the general conference.

of annual accrued interest to remain in principle, and 20% used to sustain the budget for the publications department of communications, such as the Connection Magazine and the maintenance of the Headquarters building. The standard was that ministry operations, salaries, etc., would be funded from the local church conference support. The goal was to one day fund the entire General Church from the local church conference support and free up annual endowment interest for missions. There were external funds received for publications and missions from individuals every year.

- Auditing standards in most of the individual districts failed the requirements. The General Church followed the standards, but the districts had repeated embezzlement reports with districts, youth camps, and local church funds. Clarity on governance, auditing procedures, and *Discipline* requirements were disseminated across the denomination.
- When the International Headquarters moved to Indianapolis and a new general treasurer was elected, Capin and Crouse became the auditors. The auditors, in their initial audit, gave the General Council one year to correct multiple items or they would not be our auditors. Dr. Wease ensured the General Church was in line with not-for-profit auditing standards.
- The general conference never created an organizational structure chart of governance for the general officers and general boards. The structure of the local church is not the model for the General Church. The roles of the local church and the General Church demand two different organizational models.
- The only function of the general superintendent with finances and the budget is to sign off on the audit that all bills are paid, the auditing standards followed, reserved funds accounts are correctly disbursed, and areas for improvement are addressed to be corrected. The general treasurer and the general board of finance (GBF) create, monitor, and manage budgets, expenditures, and deficits. The general superintendent attends finance meetings when requested. Stanley Morris, GBF Chair, insured a balanced budget pointing to all bills paid and a clean audit.

- The Pastor's School was created in the Atlantic District and used for all conference events, emphasizing training and ministry preparation. Such men as Dr. Dennis Kinlaw, Dr. Walter Kaiser, Dr. Robert Coleman, Dr. Victor Hamilton, Dr. Joseph Wang and others raised pastoral practice and equipping.
- The Preaching Institute focused on sermon preparation, expository methods, and the ordination vows of Word, Sacrament, and Order. Dr. Harold Thompson also taught the Ministerial Ethics course.
- Dr. Williamson and his wife Loretta focused on the 10/40 window where most people live who do not have a gospel witness. In the wake of the internet at the turn of the century, the world had doors of mission opportunities open. The EMC and OMS communicated with a group of Methodists. The latter was leaving the Upper Myanmar Methodist denomination (UMC) because of liberalism in 2000. The General Board of World Missions directed Rev. Ken Swearingen and Dr. Williamson to investigate Myanmar's (Burma) requests. The report produced recommendations to accept this group, which left the Burma liberal Methodist Church. Rev. Darothanga was their General Superintendent and represented a trained and educated clergy of men with Seminary degrees. Rev. Lal Duh Alma as the General Secretary was the first person of contact at the Yangon airport. The group is affiliated with One Mission Society and the Evangelical Methodist Church. OMS brings trainers four times a year for church multiplication, leadership, coaching, water wells, and materials for making disciples. The EMC focused on the physical buildings and water wells with one annual visit. Loretta utilized the Prayer Department, started by Leona Zehr (General Superintendent Clyde Zehr's spouse), and mobilized prayer across the denomination.
- Gilda Williamson has introduced and trained women using the OMS Dynamic Women ministry. She created *Bibles for Myanmar*, when she realized a lack of Bibles, and a ministry of food and vitamins for families.
- Dr. Williamson called for prayer and guidance when the second quadrennium began in 2003. It was clear the last four

years were fruitful for the Kingdom, but with a ceiling. In counsel with Dr. Harold Thompson, Rev Jack Conner, and Rev. James Coulston, we agreed to focus on significant growth inhibitors to avoid the denomination falling into mediocrity. Mediocrity is easily maintained but grieves the Holy Spirit. A key aspect was to prepare the EMC organizational structure for receiving UMC congregations when the divide between the progressives and conservatives would occur.

- The General Council approved presenting a one conference model to the 2006 General Conference. The presentation created a framework of regions replacing the districts and combining all district boards into one general board. Dr. Williamson preferred the Methodist model, that the EMC had initially adopted, of Eastern and Western Annual Conferences, but supported the majority. The motivation was that the majority of districts were in decline, especially the Southern District (SD). The SD requested a hold on the plan to give them two years to correct the attendance declines. A 2008 Special General Conference was approved for a decision on the proposals.
- The 2008 special General Conference narrowly declined the constitutional change for a name change to a One Conference model. The heart of the matter was the clergy and lay leaders were unwilling to abolish or change their elected positions. It reminded us of the CSF's recommendation that a merger was necessary to avoid these recurring cycles of conflict.
- Rev. Vernon Perkins and Rev. Jack Connor contacted Dr. Jun Mateo, a Filipino Nazarene church planter residing in Sacramento, CA. A relationship developed that eventually became the Asia-Pacific Conference. Dr. Mateo and his wife Marline had set up medical mission trips to their native country. They produced nine local congregations in the greater Manila area.
- The connection to Africa results from a union with Bishop Patrick Mubobo and the Change the Nations Church in Greensboro, NC. Superintendent Dr. Thompson and Pastor Brian Gordon were the contacts. Bishop Mubobo introduced

us to his Bishop, Albert Budiaki, who lived in Montreal, Canada. Bishop Budiaki was one of the four Messenger bishops who founded the Assembly of Messengers in the Congo (DRC). The CFAM conference eventually emerged with Congolese churches in Europe and the Congo. Dr. Harold Thompson and the Atlantic District affiliated with the district, and later in 2010, CFAM became a part of the General Church in the reorganization. There were several severe misunderstandings due to our cultures when we communicated. All misunderstandings and the relationships reconciled through forgiveness and a more substantial commitment to understanding the cultural issues in our American communications and African understanding. We have experienced years of peace and focused on vision and God's Will for this work of God. In the international travel of Dr. Thompson and Dr. Williamson for Africa and Myanmar they used their airline miles, hotel credits, and personal contributions to cover expenses. The Atlantic District made the heavy upfront financial investment since the General Church does not provide budget resources. Several individuals, not always EMC, have made sizable undesignated donations over the years for the international ministry to Myanmar, Africa, and Mexico.

- There were joint meetings with the Evangelical Church to discuss a possible merger with a sister denomination. The final decision was not a merger but a partnership in ministerial training that resulted in the Evangelical School of Ministry (ESOM) for training at a Master's level. We developed Memorandums of Understanding with several theological seminaries.
- The Haggard School of Ministry transformed our Course of Study for pastors into a class modules for training. A complete scope and sequence of courses for Local Preacher license The 2018 proposed Discipline Revisions required the Evangelical School of Ministry courses for the ordination Elders.
- The General Board of World Missions provided scholarships for the week of "Train and Multiply" training and cross-cultural

missions in Greenwood, IN at One Mission Society. Bishop Patrick Mubobo, leaders from Change the Nations Church, the District, along with Philippine representation of Dr. Jun Mateo.
- The title Emeritus was approved by the general conference for retiring superintendents. Rev. Jack Connor became the first Conference Superintendent Emeritus. This emeritus status was discussed and confirmed the continual of ministry in Word, Sacrament, and Order.
- The Department of Multicultural Ministry was created to educate the pastors and churches about ethnic ministry in the USA. This conviction, that God brought the world to the USA through immigration, placed evangelism at the doorstep of local churches and communities across the USA. Rev. Vernon and Ruth Perkins traveled widely, promoting this ministry to the changing populations around our churches. There were fruitful results.

2014-2018

These years produced new international ministries for the EMC and building expansion in creating the Heritage Learning Center at the Indianapolis International Headquarters. This $150,000+ state of-the-art multimedia center was built debt-free by Stanley Morris, Rev. Coulson and Dr. Williamson's fundraising efforts. The need for ministerial training in the USA and internationally was growing. A donor considered a large scholarship endowment for this ministry following the 2018 General Conference. After several years of communication and visits to the USA, a Methodist group from South Africa desired training through the online Heritage Learning Center. This group speaks English. Bishops Budiaki and Mubobo from the CFAM Conference sent delegates to the South Africa Annual Conference.

The recommendations from Christian Service Fellowship (CSF) numbers 3, 4, 5 guided the efforts for igniting growth in the denomination. The belief from our EMC founders that God brought the EMC into existence for the occurrence of the great division in the UMC between the liberals and the conservatives, motivated the denominational leadership to prepare for this historic future event. The USA landscape is filled with Methodist churches. If ignited by an outpouring of the Holy Spirit, it would bring renewal revival. The transformation would go beyond the walls of the local church into all of the USA. The First and Second Great Awakening in our US history testifies to a nation-wide outpouring of the Holy Spirit. The Wesleyan Covenant Association, being the midwife for birthing the Global Methodist Church, is playing a pivotal role.

The following list is not in sequential order of occurrence during these years 2014-2018:

- The Descriptive title International was added to the USA general superintendent to make an international ministry statement. The insertion of International was the first step toward globalization structural change for this new global world. All the general superintendents/bishops of all the conferences are international superintendents equal with mutual status. The discussion emphasized that this title is not a governance title with any authority over the international mission fields and elected officers. The international conferences and leaders are equals. The USA EMC rejects the autocratic model of being superior to our global brothers and sisters.
- The youth ministry with youth camps and district-owned campgrounds received unified support. Every district was committed to children, youth, and family camps. A few districts required the clergy to attend the week of camp stressing the importance of this ministry.
- Dr. Williamson worked during the 2014-2018 quadrennium with Dr. Jun Mateo training the pastors in the Philippines and organizing the conference for approval as a mission conference at the 2018 General Conference. There were youth retreats, School of Ministry courses, and especially church multiplication training. The General Superintendent's priorities were the training of leaders and organizing alongside Dr. Jun Mateo the churches in the Philippines, to become the new Asia Pacific Conference in 2018. Dr. Leroy Lindsay taught a class on holiness theology to the Filipino pastors; Dr. Jun Mateo and

Dr. Ed Williamson brought leadership training and pastoral classes for the ministry.
- Dr. Williamson offered to serve the 2018-2022 Quadrennium where he would focus on the CFAM Mission Conference with Bishop Budiaki and Bishop Mubobo. In the previous decade Europe and Africa was the joint priority focus for Dr. Harold Thompson and Dr. Williamson.
- The first and third Thursday every month the conference superintendents and general superintendent met virtually for prayer (first Thursday) and updates (second Thursday). A rating scale of 1 to 5 (five was the highest) was developed for the health of each local church. Each Conference Superintendent (CS) would share for each church under their care a number from one to five, five being the excellent church vitality. The ministry of the USA conference superintendents was their assigned regions and local churches in their regions.
- Conference Superintendents had two priority assignments for the 2014 to 2018 Quadrennium. If the CS failed at their assignments the church would decline in these four years. First was to promote and maintain the Natural Church Development (NCD) for growing healthy churches. Several churches had enrolled and invested in the NCD. The General Board of Evangelism had paid for the CS training at the NCD training center in Chicago. Secondly, they were to make the regions function in developing the connectional relationship between the churches. This was to include pastor and spouse retreats, training events and visiting the churches to preach the whole counsel of God to the congregations. The growth of the USA churches depended upon the success of these two priorities.
- Our 2010 new one-conference model had a known weakness and possible pitfall. The delegates of the general conference elected the conference superintendents (CS) making them accountable to the general conference, not the general superintendent (GS). The cabinet of superintendents is a programming and strategy group for planning healthy ministry for the local churches. There was still a fear that giving the general superintendent the authority to appoint

conference superintendents empowered that office with too much control in our congregational commitments. I concur with those concerns. The restructure in the one-conference model clarified a distinctive focused role of ministry for the superintendents. The CS are not members or involved in the ministry of the General Boards, so they can focus on the health of the local churches. The elimination of General Church administrative duties lessens the danger of a CS functioning as a CEO and not a shepherd to pastors and churches. We again faced the warnings of the 1976 report from CSI about weaknesses in our congregational-connectional model. The unaddressed concern was leaving the CS on the general council which creates a voting-bloc in the general council.

- The pre-conference program for the 2018 General Conference was the HOPE 61 training seminar from OMS to prevent human trafficking, mobilizing our local churches. Gilda Williamson had organized and promoted this event. The goal was for the Evangelical Methodist Women and local churches to embrace this ministry across the USA.
- The 2018 General Conference experienced strife with fears of the influx of UMC congregations and the changes this would bring to the present status quo of denominational offices. The number of new voting delegates in the new group would overwhelm the present number of voting delegates at the next general conference controlling the elections of superintendents.
- The USA churches were experiencing decline in worship attendance and a lack of healthy connectional fellowship we experienced in the past. The one-conference model, with regions, had been patterned from the Atlantic District Conference and Mid States District Conference, where there was good fellowship and cooperation among the clergy and churches. The issue was therefore not in the regional model, but in the execution of ministry and by lack of conference leadership.
- An unprecedented action passed to postpone all *Discipline* revisions, which silenced the local churches' voices who had presented their *Discipline* revisions. A consequence was the

Evangelical School of Ministry (ESOM) eventual closure, which was the partnership of the Evangelical Church and the EMC for training pastors for ministry at a Master's Degree level. The General Board of Ministerial Education had presented revisions to guarantee the survival of ESOM and educational preparation for ministry.

- The $205,000 fully furnished Heritage Learning Center built debt-free (2016) adjoined the Headquarters building in Indianapolis. It was a state-of-the-art facility for training through multimedia to the International Conferences and training for the USA local churches. They provided a place for training as needed for ESOM and Haggard School of Ministry. There were many donors. The endowment fund for training with pastoral scholarships was a $40,000 gift to be received following the 2018 General Conference.

This time frame prior to 2018 is before the Wesleyan Covenant Association was fully viable as an option for the departure.

> *The EMC was in position as a refuge and home for those seeking biblical Christianity with a Methodist heritage and connection.*

- The fulfillment of our founders' vision of the EMC being a refuge for conservative Methodists from the UMC was materializing. Dr. Williamson worked intensely with UMC pastors and churches about to exit the UMC. There was no clear establishment of what was to become the Global Methodist Church.
- In his 2018 General Superintendent's report, Dr. Williamson presented in media presentation the denomination reasons and goals in Dr. Hamblen's own words. The slow exodus that had begun from the UMC was the fulfillment of Dr. Hamblen's prophetic projections. The EMC was in a position as a refuge and home for those seeking biblical Christianity as Methodist. The solid potential for medium to large churches in Dr. Hamblen's former Texas Annual Conference to join the

EMC was announced for denomination-wide prayer. By the time of the 2018 General Conference, eight to ten churches in one Conference alone were at a point of affiliation with the EMC following the General Conference. The influx of churches would immediately change the present denomination by including new leadership and voting delegates.

- The statistical reports at the 2018 General Conference showed a loss of members and a diminished number of churches. The expansion of the ministry for local church health through the Natural Church Development died on the vine. The regions with pastor and spouse retreats and the development of the connectional fellowship among the churches failed. This church revitalization ministry's failure brought about the closing of churches. It enhanced the need for a genuine revival in our churches.

A new quadrennium with Dr. Williamson would have brought about recommendations for growing a global denomination. A draft restructuring of what the EMC could be in this new globally connected world was ready for discussion at the 2018 General Conference as a prayerful road map. As the OMS Board of Trustees chair, Dr. Williamson experienced a 12+ years transition toward making OMS international partners equals through governance training. The EMC draft included a 2020 Special Called General Conference for needed restructuring from the influx of new churches from the UMC and the election of a new General Superintendent. Dr. Williamson would have served for two years of the four-year quadrennial.

The fulfillment of our founder's vision of the EMC being a refuge for conservative Methodists from the UMC was materializing.

Dr. Williamson often stated that he envisioned a General Conference that had to postpone business because the Holy Spirit brought renewal through confession, repentance, and agape love to the delegates. A genuine revival requires repentance for the sins "in the camp" over our years of existence as a denomination. He envisioned a service utilizing John Wesley's Covenant Service, the prelude to fervent prayer and a fresh outpouring of the Holy Spirit. The possibility for the EMC to have a renewal is ever-present. An ordained Elder came to Dr. Thompson and Dr. Williamson asking forgiveness for his attitudes and actions and seeking prayer for new ministry. Confession is a good sign of the Holy Spirit's ministry among us for revival.

The new quadrennial (2018-2022) demands the leaders to lead into a new era of purpose for the denomination. Our window has closed to receive new churches from the UMC, a refuge for local churches and pastors. All efforts for a merger or educational partnership (ESOM) have failed. Why does the EMC exist beyond our purpose statements and holiness phraseology?

My brother Jack Wease would agree with me for this truth: the EMC's foundation is a passion for the world and a flame for revival. This knowledge has fueled my ministry in the EMC and sets a solid hope for the denomination's future. I love the people of the EMC, and as Dr. Hamblen stated, 'the EMC is a layman's denomination.'

Epilogue

This epilogue shares personal reflections on Covenant Church in Morgantown, WV, and a focus for the future of a global Great Awakening. The fulfillment of Dr. Hamblen's vision for a return to original Methodism and the authority of Scripture in the Methodist Church (UMC) is now deposited in the Global Methodist Church (GMC). The GMC is a genuine, emerging, global Methodist denomination.

The priority and principle for life and ministry are the Kingdom first. The Holy Spirit infuses a single-focused priority into the heart through the experience of entire sanctification. The heart is purified from self-centeredness and inward focus, not sinless performance, but perfect love for God and people. Loretta, Gilda, and myself have focused on sanctification as a whole, which fills a person with agape love for God and all people. Entire sanctification is a fresh and definite infilling of a believer with the Holy Spirit producing single-focused agape love for God and all people from all cultures and economic statuses. It is the total surrender of myself to the will of God. Purifying the heart from self-interest. Empowerment for a holy lifestyle. And participating in the Great Commission.

> *The heart has to be purified from self-centeredness and inward focus.*

The people of a local church are our Lord's bride, not the pastor's possession.

What my dad taught me from the Scripture has guided my life and decisions regarding the leading and direction of the Holy Spirit. It has reminded me of who I serve.

> "If God wants you somewhere, let Him place you" was my dad's often quoted phrase. His verse was Proverbs 18:16, "A man's gift maketh room for him, and bringeth him before great men (KJV)."

In 1968 the Evangelical United Brethren, my denomination, merged with the Methodist Church to become the United Methodist Church. I became a member of the Good News Movement for renewal in the UMC. The Good News Movement was the voice of the evangelicals seeking renewal from within the Methodist denomination. My first Master's Degree was from Gordon Conwell Theological Seminary where the leading figure of mid-20th century of American Evangelicalism was President, Dr. Harold J. Ockenga, The seminary promoted the infiltration of liberal compromised denominations in both the Reformed and Methodist traditions as the voice of orthodoxy for a return to the authority of Scripture. The goal in my denomination, the UMC, was to avoid an exodus and overcome the liberal theological liberalism for a return to original Methodism.

My second Master's Degree from Asbury Theological Seminary had the same focus for Methodism. Since I was committed to renewal from within the denomination, I studied at Boston University School of Theology, the oldest United Methodist seminary that gave a 'credibility' to my ministry among the liberal wing of the UMC in WV. The degree added to my potential usefulness for the Lord. Still, I followed my dad's advice and Proverbs in not playing the Annual Conference political game. I was told by District Superintendents how to promote myself and guarantee a good appointment for the future. They shook their heads at me because I did not follow their advice.

Loretta and I became acquainted with Dr. Dan Pacifico and his spouse Eileen at the WV United Methodist Annual Conference. We all had committed to the rebirth and renewal of the UMC by joining the Good News Chapter in the West Virginia Annual Conference. Dan and I shared a love for inductive Bible study and church multiplication. Dr. Pacifico initiated the Victory EMC in Preston County.

While serving in the UMC, a situation arose where instructions were to overlook (not accept) the evidence and knowledge of a practicing same-sex clergy member. Eventually, I refused to cover up the situation following meetings with the Board of Ordained Ministry. My request was the transfer of credentials. At that point, I did not know where I would for pastoral ministry and announced I was not available for a new pastoral appointment at the June session of the WV Annual Conference. This decision to leave the United Methodist Church was painful and grieved my heart. I had worked hard educationally and prayed intensely for the United Methodist denomination renewal for many years.

The disenchantment with the prior UMC General Conference brought many people together in North Central WV asking for a new church that would uphold the authority of the bible. Covenant Church was birthed at that time with a strong lay leadership in the Ramada Inn in Morgantown, WV. There was a definite call to plant churches in North Central WV. The church began to tithe on the newly created building fund for a future church plant on our second Sunday in the rented facility. The following Sunday, we had missionaries going to Pakistan. They became our first of several missionaries sent by the church. Covenant was living out the words of John Wesley, "...the world is my parish..." (from Wesley's Journal entry on June 11, 1739). The earliest convictions was God was calling this new church to global missions and church multiplication in WV before we owned property or a church facility.

The emerging DNA at Covenant was intentional about the children's ministry, international missions, church planting, mobilizing the laity for ministry, and biblical worship in ritual and song. The worship services and messages focused on Jesus alone and people who need the Lord. The command of the Great Commission from the Lord was 'to make disciples'. Dr. Robert Coleman, Professor of Evangelism at Asbury Seminary, used this quote of Wesley, 'converts do not change the world, disciples do'. Dr. Charles Church our District Superintendent and the EMC provided the partnership we needed for this ministry in WV.

Covenant established a policy to only support the missions in the 10/40 window where most unreached people groups lived. The first 'adopted people group' was the Uzbeks. This commitment occurred while renting from the Ramada Inn before Covenant Had a permanent home. When we affiliated with the EMC, our prayer was for the EMC to have a mission conference within the 10/40 window filled with EMC congregations.

> *"...converts do not change the world disciples do."*

The first mission in the 10/40 window did materialize until 2001 in Myanmar (Burma), with a group leaving the British Upper Myanmar Methodist Church to form the Evangelical Methodist Church of Myanmar. I wish I had time here to share with you all about the champions of this work: Rev. Darothanga, Myanmar General Superintendent, Dr. Lalduhama, Myanmar General Secretary, Rev. Ken Swearingen, chair of the General Board of World Missions, Dr. Harold Thompson, Conference Superintendent, and Rev. David Hayes, chair of the General Board of Trustees. The second international mission in the 10/40 window was the official formation of the Asia Pacific Conference with Dr. Jun Mateo in 2018.

Loretta and I had pressure from people to stay independent because they felt betrayed by the UMC. We preferred to have a Methodist connection with one of the denominations promoting Wesleyan Arminian theology and Biblical holiness in faith and practice. We looked at several, denominations including the Evangelical Methodist Church (EMC). At first, the EMC did not receive serious consideration. Among our options were the Free Methodist Church, Wesleyan Church, and smaller holiness denominations.

The EMC became our final choice primarily because of the founder, Dr. Hamblen, and his vision to be a refuge for those leaving the UMC's progressive liberal movement and the use of the original Articles of Religion from the Methodist Church written by John Wesley. The other major factor was the congregation was allowed to own their own property and had the ability to exit the denomination if the EMC's vision and biblical practices and ethics were altered in the future. The denomination has blessed Covenant, and in return Covenant has blessed the EMC.

In May 1984, we signed an Affiliation Resolution. We received $1000 from the denomination. That is the only outside funding we received in all of our years as a church. It has been a faith filled journey.

The first youth camps we participated in were with pastors Art Wilt and Jeff Williamson and their independent Cornerstone Church in Parkersburg, WV. A visit from Ricki Garner influenced Covenant to invest in Indian Cave Youth Camp. Over the years, we committed 100 percent, with thousands of dollars contributed through the people of Covenant. As a church, we Covenant received blessings upon blessings where our young people were transformed and sanctified by the Spirit.

Covenant established a fall and spring youth retreat in WV to supplement the summer youth camp at Indian Cave. The distance from the North to attend the children's camp at Indian Cave in Virginia, made it impossible to attend. A joint EMC camp with Faith Country Chapel, New Castle, PA, led by Pastor Dan Pacifico; Harvest from Jane Lew, WV, with Pastor Jeff Williamson, and Covenant on Morgantown, WV, together we establish the Children's Camp for the northern churches.

Eight churches were planted in WV from 1986 to 1998 by Covenant Church. Church multiplication became an emphasis of the District and General Boards of Evangelism where I served. Over the years, Covenant brought into the EMC a total of 12 pastors. There was no national logo, and Ron Utt (a charter member of Covenant) drew the first logo that evolved to the present-day logo over the years.

Covenant experienced its highest attendance of over 700 people in 1998. Our conviction was never to measure our success by the number of people attending, but how the people were transforming in godliness and holiness by the Word of God. We were considering a Saturday night or additional Sunday morning service in the Fall. Another option we considered was a new daughter church plant in our immediate vicinity of Morgantown. So we planted Kingdom EMC in Westover, WV in 1998. Prior to this there had been years of fervent prayer for a daughter church plant in Westover across the Monongahela River from downtown Morgantown. Covenant leaders gave experience to this newly formed church temporarily serving on the Board of Stewards as members from Covenant supported the new church. A prayer service at Covenant launched Kingdom EMC calling a former UMC pastor Rev. Kevin Cain who had assisted Dr. Dan Pacifico in our church plant in Wheeling, WV.

The most significant Covenant decision was Loretta's and my willingness and me to serve as the General Superintendent of the EMC, which required resigning from Covenant and moving to the headquarters in Indianapolis, IN. It was a momentous decision for us. My fellow pastors from across the denomination asked me if this could be God's Will as it would involve many sacrifices. There would be a significant salary cut. Loretta would have to leave Covenant Christian School. The home the Lord gave us that we had remodeled would be sold. Finally, there are no mountains in central Indiana and I had been a West Virginia mountaineer my whole life!

The more significant personal concern would be that Loretta and I would be giving up our best years for ministry, and they would not be at Covenant. We had recently turned down an appeal from David Wilkerson to return to Teen Challenge in NYC.

Over my years at Covenant, the church had given a lot to the denomination. As the General Superintendent, Loretta and I carried the same passion for Kingdom expansion, people, pastors, and their spouses. The EMC grew numerically and produced new churches. The prayer from Covenant for all those years that EMC would provide ministry in the 10/40 window became a reality with Myanmar and the Philippines (Asia Pacific Conference). The added blessing was the (Europe Africa) Canadian Conference (now CFAM) through Bishop Albert Budiaki and Bishop Patrick Mubobo. The EMC had expanded beyond North America.

Is the Lord finished with our Evangelical Methodist Church? The answer is 'no.' The Great Commission is still in effect, and the EMC needs to define its purpose within this command. The EMC denominational leadership is more than one generation removed from the influence of its founders. The danger to avoid is a veneer of biblical holiness lacking an understanding

> *The danger to avoid is a veneer of biblical holiness lacking the power and practice of 'heart purity.'*

and practice of 'heart purity.' The result is a holiness denomination absent of the Spirit's power that propelled the early Methodists across America and empowered Bishop Francis Asbury to ride on horseback 275,000 miles, sharing the whole gospel.

My prayer is for the denomination to seek God for a fresh outpouring of the Holy Spirit and for a new anointing for the EMC's denominational leadership. The Conference Superintendents, Dr. Harold Thompson, Rev. Jack Conner, and Rev. James Coulston covenanted together for the Spirit's outpouring in the EMC in our 2003 meeting mentioned earlier. We did experience growth and Kingdom expansion. We agreed to make necessary changes to remove growth inhibitors and prepare for any future influx of churches from the UMC. The prayer was for growth through conversion in the churches, anointing of the Spirit upon the preaching of the clergy and superintendents producing new converts to Christ, and for people healed from sickness and freedom from addictions.

John Wesley believed this was possible as seen in his famous quote:

> *"Give me one hundred preachers who fear nothing but sin and desire nothing but God, and I care not whether they be clergymen or laymen, they alone will shake the gates of Hell and set up the kingdom of Heaven upon Earth."* (Letter to Alexander Mather, August 6, 1777, Wesley's Letters, Volume 6)

The present-day Evangelical Methodist Church should embrace its fundamental commitments to promote holiness and evangelism. Fervent prayer will fan into flame the hot coals deposited by the Spirit in the founding of the denomination and exhibited in the founders' lives. I continue to grasp at the hope to an experience at General Conference of confession of our sins and spiritual renewal.

> *Any form of Methodism without clarity on entire sanctification has an uncertain future.*

A new purpose, mission, and reason for the denomination's existence emerging as the result.

The experience, understanding, and practice of scriptural holiness, which is the full sanctification/baptism of the Spirit, is the Methodist Church's power. Any form of Methodism without clarity on entire sanctification has an uncertain future. Justification by faith through grace is the initial sanctification, follow by a process of becoming more and more like Christ throughout our earthly life. John Wesley quotes 1 John 5:16 repeatedly in his sermon on 'Christian Perfection. *"We know that God's children do not make a practice of sinning, for God's Son holds them securely, and the evil one cannot touch them."*

The cross breaks the power of practice, 'deliberate' sinning, and transforms us from sinful practices to love for God and our neighbor. Entire sanctification is cleansing the heart from the root sin of self-interest and inward focus of entitlements to "My life...my career...my desires...my rights." A transformation from "My" to "HIS," expressed in single focused love for God and people who need the Lord. This love has no exclusions and embraces the marginalized of society, the hungry, the hurting, and the sexually confused. The overflow is the empowerment of the Holy Spirit to share the Good News of Christ and live a holy life that expresses the character of a holy God. Original Methodism proclaims everything Christ died for us to have and share with all people.

John Wesley proclaimed, "(Full sanctification) is the grand depositum (deposit) which God has lodged with the people called Methodists; and for the sake of propagating this chiefly God appeared to have raised us up." -Letter to Robert Carr Brackenbury, September 15, 1790, Wesley's Letters, Volume 7.

There is a Third Great Awakening emerging around the globe among all people groups. I believe it is the move of God to complete the Great Commission and return with a new Heaven and new Earth (2 Peter 3:13). The departure from the United Methodist, which Dr. Hamblen believed would come, has founded the Global Methodist Church (GMC) as their refuge. The impact of the Gospel through the GMC will reach every continent. All Methodist-related churches and small denominations will have a part to play in this global Great Awakening.

People who study the writings and practices of John Wesley recall the prophetic words near the end of his life:.'

Epilogue

> *I am not afraid that the people called Methodists should ever cease to exist either in Europe or America. But I am afraid lest they should only exist as a dead sect, having the form of religion without the power. And this undoubtedly will be the case unless they hold fast both the doctrine, Spirit, and Discipline with which they first set out.' ('Thoughts Upon Methodism,' 1786.)*

My prayer for our EMC is that God will save us from being ordinary with a fresh vision and a clear message of holiness in word and lifestyle.

In 2018 Gilda and I became missionaries with One Mission Society. Gilda serves with the Dynamic Women Ministries (DMW) and myself as Vice President at Large. Our specific assignments are Myanmar in the 10/40 Window where most of the unreached people in the world live. We serve as Myanmar's Church Multiplication Facilitator (CMF) and Gilda focuses on Dynamic Women Ministries with the Myanmar EMC and Myanmar Evangelical Holiness Church.

The second assignment for me is being the liaison for OMS with the Wesley Covenant Association (WCA) and the new Methodist denomination, the Global Methodist Church (GMC). My experience with a hybrid 'congregational/connectional' was shared with the leadership of the WCA. The new GMC insures the local church owns their property and has a consulting process in pastoral selection. I served on the WCA Ad Hoc Committee drafting the recommendations for local church and global mission ministries. The GMC is already a global Methodist family with thousands of members in hundreds of churches especially in Africa and the Asia Pacific region.

There is a personal direct focus on North Central WV and the future of the GMC in these WV counties. This is a return to the original vision for church multiplication producing local congregations who would be true to original Methodism as taught by John Wesley.

The GMC is a return to original Methodism in faith, practice and the empowerment of the Holy Spirit for sharing the Good News around the globe.

God is bringing a Third Great Awakening to the world prior to His return. The reignited new Methodist Church is a part of God's timing and plans to bring in a final harvest. Based on my understanding of early church history and the reports of revival and renewal, I believe Africa will be the point of spear in this fresh move of God for the world. The Methodist have a part, the GMC is focused on kingdom first in mission, along with many in the Reformed and Pentecostal traditions.

Dr. A.W. Tozer(1897-1963) impacted the last century. In 1919, five years after his conversion and without formal education in Christian theology, Tozer accepted an offer to serve as pastor of his first church, a store front in Nutter Fort, WV. That began 44 years of ministry associated with the Christian and Missionary Alliance (C&MA). Dr. Tozer gives us the prophetic word for this final Great Awakening saying a new leader must arise:

> *If Christianity is to receive a rejuvenation, it must be by other means than any now being used. If the Church in the second half of this century is to recover from the injuries she suffered in the first half, there must appear a new type of leader. The proper, ruler-of-the-synagogue type will never do. Neither will the priestly type of man who carries out his duties, takes his pay and asks no questions, nor the smooth-talking pastoral type who knows how to make the Christian religion acceptable to everyone. All these have been tried and found wanting.*
>
> *Another kind of religious leader must arise among us. He must be of the old prophet type, a man who has seen visions of God and has heard a voice from the Throne. When he comes (and I pray God there will be not one but many), he will stand in flat contradiction to everything our smirking, smooth civilization holds dear. He will contradict, denounce and protest in the name of God and will earn the hatred and opposition of a large segment of Christendom. Such a man is likely to be lean, rugged, blunt-spoken and a little bit angry with the world. He will love Christ and the souls of men to the point of willingness to die for the glory of the One and the salvation of the other. But he will fear nothing that breathes with mortal breath."* (A.W. Tozer, The Size of the Soul, 128-129)

Dr. Vanderwood, Dr. Hamblen

Dr. Williamson

Dr. Lucian Smith and Dr. Hamblen, 1953

Rev. Gordon Johnson and Rev. Jimmy Mumme

General Superintendents Dr. Williamson (International)
and Rev. Cardenas (Mexico)

Eastern Annual, 1955

Dr. J.H, Hamblen

Rev John Banks, Dr. JH Hamblen, Rev. Jack Wease, Rev. Carl Main

Texas Conference, 1952

Bishop Patrick Mubobo & Bishop Albert Budiakai -
Christ for All Nations (CFAN)

Dr. Charles Church, Atlantic District Superintendent

Dr. Hamblen (USA) and Dr. Vargas (Mexico) General Superintendents

EMC leaders

Rev. John and Mable Kunkle

Founding Leaders, 1947

First Class of Deacons, 1946

Western Annual Conference, 1967

Dr. C.P. Haggard

Eastern Annual Conference, Scio, NY

Rev. Darothanga, Myanmar General Superintendent and Rev. Kenneth Swearingen, USA Chair of the General Board of World Missions.

www.ingramcontent.com/pod-product-compliance
Lightning Source LLC
LaVergne TN
LVHW041542060526
838200LV00037B/1096